Praise for Soul Su. . . . . ui

Mandy Kocsis has a unique writing style that sets her apart from others. And her book, SOUL SURVIVOR is no different. From the opening piece, THE HAUNTING, to the last line of the book's final piece, CATASTROPHIC, you are seeing tales of life and love through Mandy's eyes.

She brings you into her world as only she can. Pieces like SOUL DANCING really touch on how life sometimes takes us down paths which cause us to lose our joy, no matter how hard we try to fight it. Mandy uses her words to spin every type of emotion with her poetic storytelling and pieces like THE WOMAN YOUR MOTHER NEVER THOUGHT OF, will have you walking right alongside her through the journey.

Overall SOUL SURVIVOR has 142 entries, all worthy of the ink that's been spilled to write them. I'd say Mandy Kocsis has put together a wonderful collection and it makes a great addition to any poetry collection.

Jay Long, author of *Eternal Echoes*

This book is amazing. It left me speechless. The way she captures the words in THIS book, makes you feel it deep down to your bones. It is pure magic.

Mandy has a true writers gift. Soul Survivor is the perfect name for this book, because that's exactly what Mandy is. She has written a survival guide for those who have gone through similar events, reminding us that life is nothing more than a poetic journey of survival... and it is nothing short of amazing.

B. Vigil, author of *Beauty in Darkness*

Mandy Kocsis' SOUL SURVIVOR is a journey of one woman's pain and survival. You will find yourself breathing in every word, feeling every emotion rise and fall in your chest. You will be drawn into her world of words spilled onto the pages. Her poems are the breath you needed, but was unable to express. She brings it all to life with eloquence and a gentle touch. Her strength is a guiding light through a journey of darkness. Every poem is a layer of her soul being pulled back, revealing every wound, every scar. You will feel you are not alone, finally understood in this sometime upside down world. SOUL SURVIVOR is a compass for surviving, but is also the first step on a path to healing and finding peace.

April Y. Spellmeyer, author

Soul Survivor

Mandy Kocsis

blank
paper
press

Michigan

For information, address Blank Paper Press at
kindramaustinauthor@gmail.com

Published in the United States of America by
Blank Paper Press.

blank
paper
press

Michigan

ISBN: 978-1-7328610-6-0

Dedication

For my mom and my son,
Always my biggest fans.
And for Jeff B. Buchin...
The one who got away,
But will always be here, in my ink.

Here's to the difference
Between survival and existence.

I love you all.

Acknowledgements

Cathy Oliver - without whom I'd have stopped writing at 15. I love you.

Stacy Embry-Nation - my first co-author...from forever ago until forever is gone...I love you

Erika Amerika: I DID IT!!! NO TINY MURDERS!!! Mew!!!

Gerry Hanna - without whom none of this would've been possible. I love you, mate.

Kindra Austin: ALLLL the reasons. And then some. I love you!!!

Angie Waters: your amazing cover art blows me away! Thank you, soooo much!!! I love you!!!

April Spellmeyer: thank you for always being there. For your beautiful words on the back of this book. I love you.

Alfa Holden: Thank you for believing in me. For being such an amazing person and dear friend. I love you.

Jay Long: thank you for being a friend when not many were. For not letting me give up. Thank you for your beautiful advanced review. I love you.

Brianna Vigil: thank you for understanding my darkness, and being brave enough to join me there a time or two lol. Thank you for the beautiful review. I love you.

Hunter-Man: what can I say? Thanks for the best conversation EVER. Cosmic twins till the end!!! I love you!

And to the rest of my Warrior Soul Sisters...
Thank you. I love you.

Contents

Soul Survivor

The Haunting

They're the ones that haunt you at night.
The ones you couldn't save;
Though you tried with all your might.

Especially that one you avoid seeing in the mirror...
Because no matter what you did,
You still didn't save her.

Twilight Child

Night was falling on her soul
But there was no one left to tell
A twilight child all her life
She was falling down a well
And she knew no one would catch her
And she knew that she was lost
And she couldn't find much will to care
If the price was worth the cost
Some things you can't escape from
And sometimes you're better off
Falling through the darkness
With no clue how you'll stop
Than clinging to a crumbling ledge
That refused to hold you up.

When I Was 6 Years Old

So much, she was bleeding,
But her heart, it was beating.
I could tell she was breathing,

And I knew she was dead.

I thought that the screaming was inside my head…

I don't think I've ever stopped.
She survived, I thank the Gods,
She survived…but parts of me did not.

The Forgotten One

I am the thought they leave behind
The wish they never make
I am the nightmare to their dreams;
The one they push away.
And that's okay,
Because it's always been that way.
I'm used to it…
And only cry in written ways.

The Lioness

You shattered the girl I was
Like so much glass, she broke
Yet, in a fucked up way, I thank you
For in the breaking you provoked
The Lioness I was always meant to be.

The Lost

It took a look to fall for you
And 14 years to crash
That was one hell of a death drop
A long and bloody splash
Truth is, it's not so recent,
I landed long ago
Took a little longer to expel
That last breath we call hope
Now I begin the healing
And the damage that you caused
In flying high, I'll find my sky,
And you're the one that lost.

Dirty Girl

She's a dirty girl in a Windex world
Where there are no shades of gray
And she could go so far in life
But her zip code's in the way
People see what they want to see
So she's just her surface to the world
They don't see her soul is clean;
To them, she's just a dirty girl.

Diamond-Dipped Cyanide

They thought she was steel and roses, but her soul was diamond-dipped cyanide. Beautiful to look at, but deadly to touch. She wanted it that way. She would destroy love itself before ever letting it destroy her, again.

Fallen Angels

Who are you, to demand perfection?
Even angels fall sometimes.

Scathing

(An Acrostic Poem)

Screaming inside, just
Can't stop
Aching soul
Tears me up
Hell on Earth
Inside myself
Never ending
Gut-wrenching stuff.

Psychotic Merry-Go-Round

Up, down, up, down
My life's a psychotic merry-go-round
Can't win for losing
Can't lose to win
Try to do right
Like an angel that sins
My soul's on my sleeve
My heart's at its last
I can't win for losing;
I'm spinning too fast.

The Dime

People often say, "we are not promised tomorrow"
And that's true.
We're not.
Hell, we're not even promised today.
Still, every day we go about our lives,
Dreaming dreams and making plans.
Some of us with the full and complete knowledge
That life can turn on a dime.
We've answered those middle-of-the-night phone calls
That change everything.
We've opened the doors that can never be closed.
We know.
WE KNOW.
Yet, somehow, as years pass between events,
We start living again.
Dreaming again.
We make promises of forever
Knowing there's no such thing.

Until life drops that dime, again.

This time, it's sudden and slow
All at once.

It's watching that dime fall in slow motion
Then bounce repeatedly
In even slower time.
Knowing that when it does finally cease all movement
Your life is going to be changed forever.
YOU'RE going to be changed.
And the whole time you're watching the silent
Stop-motion of life's dime
You're wondering if you'll even survive it.
Knowing you won't want to. Knowing you've
GOT to.
Somehow.
This is my story.
I'm watching this dime fall from the hand of fate
So slowly, and too quickly, all at once.
Knowing what these days truly are:
The changing of everything.

Death and Darkness

I'm not afraid of Death.
I've done it.
I've seen the other side.
I'm afraid of falling so deep into my Darkness
That I never live while I'm alive.

Daymares

The pain inside is so intense
I can't speak and I can't rest
Liquid fire in my veins
Enough to kill the sanest sane
Nightmares, daymares, bill the light
I took a chance and lost the fight.

Nightmares

The hour is late
There's no-one around
Nothing but silence;
There's no other sound.
Awakened in darkness
From blood-coated dreams
Still "hearing" the nightmare;
The most silent of screams.
Eyes darting quickly,
Unsure if I slumber
While throughout my body
My heart violently thunders.
The shadows seem living
As I creep from my bed
While echoes of nightmares
Replay in my head.
I tiptoe in silence
Inspecting my home
Each door, lock, and window
To ensure I'm alone.
Yes, the hour is late,
There's no-one around
Nothing but silence;
There's no other sound.

The Graveyard of My Dreams

Walking after midnight
Past the graveyard of my dreams
So much, now, lays buried there
So many shattered things…

A little girl who bounced and twirled
Who saw the best in all the worst
In the graveyard of my dreams,
She was buried, first.

A little wild teenaged child
Who lived her life with flair
In the graveyard of my dreams
She, too, lies resting there.

Just another forgotten mother
Grieving for her past
In the graveyard of my dreams
She was buried last.

Drifting after midnight
Past the graveyard of my dreams
Not much more than spirit, now
Life took all I was from me.

Center Stage

My Darkness is creeping close, tonight
It wants to come and play
It longs to pull me under
Through scenes of yesterday
My room's lit up like center stage
While silence plays the score
I've lived this scene each night for years
It doesn't faze me anymore
It's when it pulls me, screaming
From dreams I can't control
That is where my darkness wins
And I fall, crying, to the floor.

Don't Forget

Don't forget the nights of tears, or the nights of blood.
Don't forget the sounds bones make as they're breaking.
Don't forget the hits to my soul;
Words like knives that carved me whole.

When you're looking in his eyes, and believing his lies,
Remember:

I learned from the best to be heartless. I learned from the
Best to be cold.

I learned from him.

Hell Survivor

They'd think my life was fiction
And, to them, they'd be right
After all, it's "just not possible"
To have survived my life.
I can't count all the traumas
Well, I could, but I won't
The times I could have slipped away
Into the Great Unknown.
I could tell one of the times I did
I could paint poetry of the scene
But what I saw on the
Other Side Was meant for only me.
So folks can think it's fiction
Just words strung together well
But what they think means nothing
To one who's already survived Hell.

Soul Dancing

They say she danced into the world
Like a supernova star
But by the time I knew her
She had fallen oh, so far
She'd learned when she was very young
Not every soul should dance
And yet it didn't stop her
Every time she had the chance
But the music, it grew darker
Smothering her soul
So that by the time I knew her
She wasn't dancing anymore
Her smile never reached her eyes
Twin oceans filled with pain
I wish I could have helped her
Find her dance, again
Instead I watched her dying
A bit more every day
Fading in the mirror
Until her soul just danced away.

Ashes

The loneliness inside my soul
Speaks of bridges burned
I'm not the one who lit the flames
I just watched the ashes churn
I know, someday, they'll all come back
I know, someday, they'll learn
The Earth will keep on spinning
And the Wheel of Fate will turn
Where they go from here on out
Is no longer my concern
I have no time for their regrets
To my life I must return.
Until the day She calls me home
Leaving ashes in an urn
Perhaps that's all there'll be to find
Amongst the bridges that they burned.

Scars

Don't pretend to know me
Because you've seen some of my scars
When you don't know how I got them
Or how they've gotten me this far
Don't think to understand me
You haven't seen how much has died
Or understand the fatal scars
Can't be seen from the outside.

The String

Dangling from a puppet string
Dancing with regret
Hanging from a golden ring
Of things I can't forget
Like distant dreams of days gone by

~ FADE TO BLACK & WHITE ~

Silent screams and tears I cried
When darkness stole my light

Of standing, silent, at her grave
When angels took my baby home
Trying so hard to be brave
As I buried her, alone
Then, fast-forward 16 years
Another nightmare made in Hell
He took my kids and disappeared
And took my light, as well
3 children to the hands of Fate
Life took away from me
I learned my lessons far too late
And so very far from free

There are so many things I'd change
If I could just go back
So many things I'd rearrange
But it's far too late for that.

Under Construction

She tried to get away
But there was nowhere left to run
She tried to pull herself together;
She'd already come undone.
The wall she'd built around her soul
Exploded into dust
Burying her in deep regret
That she had dared to trust.
And when she looked into his eyes
She knew that she was lost
She'd given him her everything
And then she paid the cost.
He'd told her that he loved her
She dared to believe
Then he left her broken
Buried, bleeding like a sieve.
So when the darkness came at night
As she lay in her empty bed
She'd given him her zest for life
Which he stabbed and left for dead.
She gathered rocks around her
And the dust; she took it all
Tempered it with steel regret;
She then rebuilt her wall.

The Broken Kind

This searing pain is killing me
Drilling through my soul
When I come out the other side
I'll be broken kind of whole.

Shattered Love

I'm breaking in silence
So nobody hears
My soul's tortured screams
My heart's bloody tears
I'm lost in this darkness
Nobody can see
I'm drowning as quickly
As your love for me
I've shattered so sharply
Pieces no one can touch
Forever alone
Because I'll never trust
Love again.

Contradictions

Silence defines me more than words
And darkness is my light
I'm a book of contradictions
Written by the night
I let few people close to me
Though many think they are
They're lost in their realities
While I'm lost among the stars.

Consumed

As poets, as writers, we purge our pain with words.
We reach through our personal parcels of hell,
Dragging the bottom of our souls,
Pulling out the bodies for the world to consume,
Before we're consumed, instead.

Sometimes, we even succeed.

Depression

(An Acrostic Poem)

Drowning in
Emptiness in
Pools of violent
Rain
Endings surround you
So much bloody pain
Somehow each day you fight
It; the urge to just give in
Over and over and over again
Never letting on; hiding behind a smile.

Mandy Kocsis

Wonderland

Oh, Dear Child…
God's not dead!!!

He saw what you were becoming,
And came to Wonderland, instead.

Stillness

(Acrostic Poem)

Sometimes
Things change
In a blink of
Lying eyes
Leaving
Nothing
Ever as it was
Stay in the
Stillness…and breathe.

Words Like Knives

The scars on my soul are just beneath skin.
When you use your words like knives,
Just know I bleed to death, again.

Judgement Day

I've looked Evil in the eye while it said
"I Love You."
As I inhaled the breath it expelled.
I've felt my heart beat beneath its defeat;
I've battled my way out of Hell.
So, while you sit there in Judgement upon me,
And preach about "God's reasons for all"
You'd better think twice, and ask your God for advice
Lest your number's the NEXT Evil calls.

Cheers!

Here's to the words you'll never say out loud
Because no air is heavy enough to hold them.

Life & Death

Staring at Death's Darkness
An Abyss, but not Oblivion
Where you think life is living
To me, Death is all we're living in
From the moment we start breathing
Whether we know it or not
The Fates have finished Weaving
And Death knows what time we've got.

Brokenness

The only "ness" I possess is brokenness;
I once was so much more
Each time I try to deal with this
Life knocks me to the floor.
Truth is, I'm tired of trying; I'll never again be whole
And what good is surviving with pieces
Missing from your soul?

Same Hell

It's a difficult thing,
To acknowledge that the Hell someone gave you
Is the same Hell that made you.

Freedom

It took me an incredibly long time to realize that there was
Too much
water under a bridge that I had burned years ago.
That I was, in fact, drowning in it.
There's a beautiful peace that comes with letting go…
Either you fall, or you fly.
You live, or you die.
Either way,
You're finally free.

Pain-dipped Skin

I'm just pain that's dipped in skin
Regret and loss and painful sin
No room for more than that, within
Angels fall and I can't win.

Inner Demons

I've never had a soft soul;
Since birth, I've done hard time
Best not meet me at my worst...
Or the demons that I hide.

Change

Standing on the precipice
Of it's all gonna change
Knowing, on the other side,
You'll never be the same
Staring at the starless sky
Holding back the fear
Praying, when it's over,
You haven't disappeared;
Swallowed whole by your abyss
Falling through the dark
Praying parts of you survive
Your soul…if not your heart.

Ghosts

Nights are the hardest, but nobody knows
Just how deep my nightmare goes.
I fear sleep like a child fears ghosts
Because mine are there, when my eyes close.

PTSD: Inside My Mind
(Acrostic Poem)

Paranoia
That's been
Steeped in heavy
Doses of Reality.

It's not about what "might" happen; it's about what DID happen.

Mandy Kocsis

Demons and Angels

He's just a man who let his demons change my soul...
And I'm just an angel with no wings to make me whole.

48

Another Life (That Isn't Mine)

My soul is tired
Perhaps it's time
To lay down and dream
A better life than mine,
A life where love
Has no price
And helping others
Has no thoughts, twice,
A life where illness has no place
And hatred has left
The Human Race
Where flowers grow
And the sun just shines
In some other life
That isn't mine.

Best Friends

Somewhere in the dark rain
I lost my rainbow's end
But, stumbling through the darkness,
The dark became my friend
There's silver linings everywhere
If you just look and think
I may have lost my rainbow's end
But I wouldn't change a thing
It's made me who I am, today;
This journey with the dark.
I may have lost some Lost Fool's Gold
But I'm best friends with the stars.

Unicorn

(An Acrostic Poem)

Until humanity finds their humanity
Never will
I claim to be
Constructed of their
Openly hate-filled
Reality
Never will that be me.

The Last Word

You changed my soul; you turned it cold.
I'll never forgive you for that.

Wings

They tried to steal my thunder
The song that my soul sings
They tried to hold me under
Not knowing I had wings.

Enlightened Darkness

Is this the way it happens?
To go from light into the dark?
The ones you love, one by one,
Dim the switches to your heart?
When life's bitter disappointments
Are all you've ever known
The dark becomes a comfort
You can't see how you're alone
Until, in pain, you find yourself
REACHING for the dark
Using it to shield you…
From how broken you really are.

Given

If not this, than that
Tit for tat
Take and take
And don't give back
Hearts get broken
And dreams go black
When love is given;
Not given back.
Insanity, quickly
Becoming fact
When all you need
Is all you lack
Pain permeating
Every crack
When love is given
But not given back.

Mandy Kocsis

Walls

I need a way out
There's no doors to my walls
No windows to see
If I'll fly, if I'll fall
I need a way free
From this nightmare I'm in
Except, I'm awake…
I can't wake, again…

Karma

Karma catches up with you
Uncaring if you weep
Balancing the scales you tip
When dancing in the deep.

The Soul

Would that the soul be split in two
When death blows still the morning dew
When breath is shallowed one last time
When life is done and left behind
Would that the soul could go, yet stay
To eternity, yet by you lay
Flying free from life's hard chains
Yet holding on to love's remains
Would that the soul be split in two
When death comes calling mourning's hue
When eternal slumber dreams arrive
Flying forth, yet by your side
I would never leave you, heart
My soul would stay, yet do depart
When breath is shallowed one last time
When life is done and left behind
Would that the soul be split in two
I would fly…yet stay…with you.

For My Children

The Missing

It occurred to me that I'm never going to see you, again
Life felt so much more like death, just then.

Weeds of Glass

I don't want your love
If love's not in your soul
I don't need you to complete me
I'm too broken to be whole
My pieces are what make me
They tell the story of my past
So if you're going to love me
Love ALL my broken glass
Sometimes I might cut you
And most times my heart just bleeds
I'm not a fragile flower, dear,
I'm the broken, growing weeds
So may tried to kill me
And all I am, inside
They just scattered glass upon the wind
And they're the ones that died.

Silver Lining

I'm drowning again
As I grasp a silver lining
At least I can spin poetry
And birth beauty from this pain.

The Line

My heart's a little shattered, now
My heart's a bloody mess
That this is where we'd go to die
I never would've guessed.
You crossed a line, can't be undone
You broke me right in two
You keep your light,
I'll be just fine
In my darkness without you.

Witch's Brew

I'd gladly drink the witch's brew
The poison to forgetting you
The apple that brings endless sleep
For every single day I weep
Don't wake me with a loving kiss
Unless loving doesn't hurt like this.

Not An Option

Giving up is not an option
Though I want to, every day
The pain in my soul is killing me
Each morning more than yesterday
I should be used to being hated
I've not been loved since my first breath
What I'd give to just not care
And how I pray there's peace in death.

Survivor's Guilt

When you're feeling creative
But all you create
Are tears for a past full of lies
You can't hit rewind
It's like losing your mind
To know you're the one that survived.

Truths From a Deaf Girl

If I gained all my hearing tomorrow
I think your world would drive me insane
I think my soul would bleed to death
Beneath the sound of all the hate.

Dark Space

When she goes into her dark space
It's best to let her roam
She'll either run herself insane…
Or she'll write her way back home.

That Evil White Rabbit

He not only didn't run from her darkness,
He followed her into her abyss.
He not only didn't try to talk her out of it,
He walked with her through it.
You see, he knew a bit about demons like hers
And damned if he was going to let them dim her light.

My Last

I will never "get over you"
As the romantics do define
But scars will grow,
And this pain will go
As all I need is time
I've survived so very much
And I've stood o'er many graves
I refuse to let love kill me
I won't go out this way
40 years behind me
And far too many yet
No, I never will "get over you"
I'll just make myself forget
Except those rare and magic nights
I'll allow myself a peek
At the memories I'll have locked away
Of a time I'll never speak
And then, someday, I'll be old and gray
I'll gather up the past
Lay down with it one more time
I'll softly breathe my last
And finally get over you.

In My Dreams

I'll see you in my dreams tonight
And it will be enough
At least there I can pretend
What you felt was really love
I can feel your arms around me
And be at home again
My heart can calm within me
My soul can breathe, and then
I'll wake up in the morning
And kiss my dreams goodbye
And pretend that everything's okay
Until I next close my eyes.

The Woman Your Mother Never

Thought Of

I am the Woman
Your mother never thought of
A Frankenstein monster
Stitched together with trauma and tears
Holding a Darkness; my greatest strength
The one who'll take a bullet
And annihilate the shooter
In one fell sweep
I am the Woman
Who bleeds in truthful ink
Who found her voice
After nights spent drowned in blood
Who clawed her way back to life
When there wasn't much worth living for
Who cries each night
Over the graves in side my soul
I am the Woman who holds on
When everyone else lets go
A Woman your mother wouldn't know
I'm the Woman who survives.

Mosaic Soul

Shattered and broken
Again and again
Glued back together
With heartache and sin
I'm just a mosaic
Sometimes I glow
And, others, I'm darkness
A mosaic soul.

Where There's Dark, There's

Light

Her darkness was hypnotic
You couldn't help but stare
So caught up in its movements
You missed what else was there.

A light so blindingly beautiful
That it scattered into stars
Damn near Supernova
But you missed it in her dark.

You could watch her for a lifetime
And still you'd never know
A single thing about her
Because you're missing half her soul.

Darkness of a Fallen Star

I never asked you to love me
And that's something you forget
I've only asked for honesty
Since the moment we met
I never asked for sunshine
Just the storm clouds in your eyes
For upon the darkest thunder
Is where I learned to fly
I never asked for anything
Even resembling forever
Just the moment in the night
When our souls come together
I'm not any girl you've ever known
I'm unique to my very soul
I'm the darkness of a fallen star
That fell long, long, ago.

Anyway

He mended her heart
Tended her soul
But some things are too broken
For love to make whole
She is who she is
And who she'll remain
Broken and glued together all wrong
Dancing just this side of sane
And he loves her, anyway.

Empty Stars

I wished upon an empty star
Unbeknownst to me
It's magic long departed
The soul inside set free
I walked upon a painful path
That seemed to have no end
Until you stepped from the shadows
And gently took my hand
And from that moment forward
I've never walked alone
Since that star I thought so empty
Took my hand and walked me home.

Ghost Dance

I'd have loved you forever
If given the chance
But you killed those dreams
And ghosts?

They don't dance.

Insomnia

I'm so tired, but I can't sleep
My soul has secrets
My heart can't keep.

Intimate Silence

Silence; it envelopes my world.
I'm comfortable with silence; intimate, even.

But on nights like this, silence is my worst enemy.
Nights I wake, throat raw from my own screams,
Tears of liquid midnight soaking my cheeks and
Staining my soul. Shadows drip like molten blood,
And there is nowhere to hide.

My past has found me, once again.

While the silence screams my many failures,
And echoes with your absence.

My demons are awake, now.

Beauty in Darkness

She's beauty in darkness
With a soul of pure light
A raven-winged angel
Born from the night
She's warmth and she's kindness
A full moon made of love
Not a star could outshine her
From the darkness above.

Darkness Dreams

For she had seen the promises
The Universe had made
She saw the glow from galaxies
Not even time could fade
It came to her in beauty
It came to her in pain
It came to her in every word
She bled onto the page
And she felt sad for those who couldn't
Or wouldn't try to see
There's so much more to everything
Even Darkness has a dream.

Lost Queen

She dressed in jewels of kindness
Though she lived a lonely life
Cloaked in ancient memories
Of a far more different time
She dreams the dreams that are no more
Just obsession with her past
A passion for dark melodies
When love was meant to last
A Queen of quiet reverie
she moves with silent grace
Well aware she's out of touch
For, here, she has no place
A heart like hers (that loves so much)
Loyal, strong, and kind
Was never meant to flourish here
She's a Queen who's lost in time.

A Thousand Goodbyes

She sweeps the stars from the skies
Drapes them over her eyes
To blind herself from the pain
Of a thousand good-byes.

Ghost Girl

The price isn't worth the cost
The love isn't worth the loss
Life is for the living
Not a girl who's just a ghost
And there's no one left to see it
The darkness taking me
And there's no one who believes it
Because there's no one here with me
Someday I'll just vanish
Swallowed by my dark
It might take my life and dreams
But it will never take my heart
So if I'm suddenly gone one day
If I lose this endless war
Please know I'm just so tired
I've been fighting for so long
I've given all I had to give
Until everything was gone
And love is not the answer
And hope is just a dream
And life is just a battle zone
And my soul is made of screams
The price I've paid was just too much

Soul Survivor

Everything I've lost
And I might seem like living
But I'm a girl who's just a ghost.

Writers

We turn time to poetry
We make our pain our rhymes
We write of better futures
While we dream of better times
Painful pasts, we turn to beauty
Our words become our fighters
In this way we'll survive death
Because, my darling, we're the writers.

*For All My Writers,
Family and Friends*

The Price

My art is my rock
My sanity, my safety
It allows me to create
And be myself

But it comes with a price.

Pouring pain to paper
Bleeding from my soul
Doubled over screaming...

And I wouldn't change it for the world.

Co-Written with Jeff B. Buchin

Mandy Kocsis

Transaction: Goodbye

I don't control
Where the words go
I just put pen to paper
And bleed from my soul
It's a painful transaction
But this much I know
You'll always remember
What you couldn't hold
And the distance between us
In a town small as this
Might one day be as close
As a butterfly's kiss
And when that day comes
I'll look in your eyes
Like I never knew you
And just walk on by
You can't even protest
What you know to be true
I'm the only one better
At goodbye than you.

Brutal Honesty

I stopped speaking my truth long ago
Most don't care, and will never know
The strength it took just to survive
To get away still so alive
My heart a shattered, useless mass
Beating wildly within my chest
In ways that most will never know
My body lived, but he killed my soul
I stopped speaking my truth long ago.

Mandy Kocsis

A Pentameter of Painful Truths

I've learned to be more quiet
About the dreams I'm letting die
I've learned to just be silent
About what's killing me inside
I've learned to fight my battles
Between the margins and the lines
A pentameter of painful truths
That want to break my mind.

90

Darkness & Light: A Collaboration

"I don't have virtues, I have victims,"
Said the darkness to the light
What he failed to understand
Was how she craved the night.
Perhaps that was the reason
She couldn't get it right
He'd never come to understand
The love that lived in light.

Co-Written with Jeff B. Buchin©2017

Bleeding

I cut people off
Seemingly without a thought
I've been told I'm heartless
That they're most likely better off
What people fail to understand
Is how it cuts me to my soul
Every time I have to do it
Less of me is whole
I think of some of them every day
I likely always will
I bleed with pain from their mistakes
When I'm moving, when I'm still
It doesn't really matter, see?
They left me no recourse
It was either cut them off
Or keep bleeding from the source.

Dream Catcher

If I fall into my nightmares,
Will you catch me in your dreams?

I Complete Me

I might be broken
Might be in pieces
I'm a beautiful mosaic
Baby, I've got this.

Empathy

I don't want to feel your pain
At times, it's just too much
Still, it lets me close to you
In ways unknown by touch
We've both been through so very much.

He Holds My Demons

He picks up the pieces of my nightmares
And holds my demons back to sleep.

Take Your Chances

Maybe I'm insensitive, maybe I'm insane
Roll the dice; take your chances
Maybe I'm humane.

Life Tried

You see, life tried to drown me in my struggles and despair
But she's tried this shit, before, and I'm still breathing air
Stronger than I used to be when life first held me down
She can give me all she's got, and I'll still stand my ground.

Spinning Stars

Spinning words into constellations;
Making poetry into stars.
When she's staring into space
She's creating her own Mars
When she puts her pen to page,
Her world becomes ours
Taking us away to somewhere
Better than where we are.

Dark-Diamond Dust

If they can't see your beauty, the dark diamond that you are,
They need not see your facets;
That you're as bright as any star.
Don't let them dim your darkness,
It's a light all on its own…
You've one of the brightest souls the world has ever known
Some will never understand, no matter how you try
There's more sparkle in dark-diamond dust
Than all the glitter in the sky.

Facets

She's got the strength of diamonds inside her soul,
With facets few will ever know.

Eclipse

Darling, he's just one star, in one galaxy,
Destined to have one moment to shine in your life.
He's had that moment.

You are the moon, darling.

Eclipse him.

Different Stars

A love story for the ages;
It exists, now, just in pages.
In vodka-drenched notes on an old guitar.
In poetry, and melodies;
Silent dreams, and memories.

In another life.

With different stars.

The Damaged

He brought me into his arms, and showed me the worth
of my heart.
It takes my breath away, and all I can think is, thank
you…
For daring to love the damaged.

The Lonely

I am still again
Watching with concrete eyes
Women I never could have been
See me
Only
As a monument for the otherwise
And I am lonely
Here in this public park.

More than just silent
My soul has gone still
Heavier than all
That carries the world
I've become a monument
Made from their tears
Silent screams; broken wings
The nightmares from their fears
And no one can see me
Because nobody looks
Outside of themselves
From the deaths life took
So while the sun shines
Here I stand in the dark

Mandy Kocsis

I'm made from the lonely
Left in each public park.

Co-Written with Kindra M. Austin

The Hourglass

Wish I could be as algid
As those who came before
Instead, I'll pay for their mistakes
While my heart breaks all the more.
A spindrift of emotion
In a hurricane of thought
Spinning 'round an hourglass
Full of dreams I - almost - caught.

Dark Fairy Tales

Even the darkest of fairy tales
Have the brightest of streams
The most whimsical loves
And the most potent of dreams.
Twisting, turning,
Truth and lies
Knives stab your heart
While love blinds your eyes.
Till there's nothing to say
Not even a grave
Just a period to a sentence
You gave your all to save.
Watch for the blood trail
Your soul's bleeding rends
Your story, now over,
The dark fairy tale ends.

Fallen Star

I never asked you to love me
And that's something you forget
I've only asked for honesty
Since the moment we met
I never asked for sunshine
Just the storm clouds in your eyes
For upon the darkest thunder
Is where I learned to fly
I never asked for anything
Even resembling forever
Just the moments in the night
When our souls come together
I'm not any girl you've ever known
I'm unique to my very soul
I'm the darkness of a fallen star
That fell long, long ago.

Nevermore

Nevermore shall I love again
And nevermore will love break me
I'll rise stronger than the strongest of Ravens
With a darkness that might actually save me.

Never will I stand there, bleeding
A tell-tale heart, dying from their deceiving
With gaping wounds to deep to be seen
For nevermore will I love.

I've come to understand, you see
Some things in life aren't meant for me
I've loved with a love that was more than love
And now I'll love the memory
But nevermore will I love.

I'll rise like the Raven and never look back
With wings to match the darkest black
And eyes that see the smallest lie
At home in the darkest midnight sky
And nevermore will I love.

Deserve Me

My heart is by invitation only, and once that's been
rescinded
There's no getting it back.
I'm not a trusting person by nature;
Made even less so by life.

You've got to deserve me.

The Toll

Like rain, tears fall in her soul
She'll not be free, and never whole
The cost is high, but no one knows
And with herself, she pays the toll.

Redemption

One mile from Redemption
With just your ghost and your guitar
Empty dreams and broken seams
Have gotten me this far
Gonna leave your ghost behind me
Wherever I might roam
At Redemption's county line
I'll retake my soul.

Broken Soul

I've come to decide I'll never be whole
I'm just an exposed heart with a broken soul.

Killing You

When there's no tears left to cry
And you're feeling dead inside
When life feels like a hopeless cause
And you'd do anything to just hit pause
Close your eyes and sleep, my dear
Dream of a better place than here
For sleep is the only true escape
Besides death, and that must wait
There's too much left that you must do
Even if it's killing you.

Daring To Believe

The pain inside; it suffocates.
But I refuse to let my heart break.
Still, I can feel those claws rake,
Down through my soul, I'm bleeding
I'm running from this feeling.
Running out of time and breath,
Can't get away; there is no rest.
Sirens blaring in my mind;
I should've known I'm not that kind.
The kind that's loved,
The kind with worth,
Feels like I'm getting what I deserve…

For daring to believe.

Moon Made

I'll never be who they want me to be
I'll never match their plan
That's okay; the moon made me
And She loves me for who I am.

Unteachable

You can't teach a person
Who's afraid of the dark
How to live in it.

The Cost

I had my time in the spotlight
Discovered I belong in the dark
Doesn't mean I don't remember;
Doesn't mean it didn't break my heart.
Up on stages nationwide
In front of countless screaming fans
I'm happiest in the shadows
As long as you're holding my hand
Feels like you're slipping away from me
Feels like I'm all alone, again
Drowning in this darkness
Don't have the strength to stand
I'm stronger than I think I am
I know this to be true
I can survive the strongest storm…

But can I survive you?

Contradictions

She's whiskey & velvet
She's cotton, she's gin
Everywhere you'll ever go
And where you've never been
You'll not understand her
To be perfectly clear
She's a woman of candor
You'll not always hear
But if you've strength to love her
For all she is and is not
She'll take you to Heaven
Or as close as anyone's got.

Paintbrushes

Stop painting me with the same brush
As the women who came before me.
Acrylics and watercolors are both paints,
But still very different things.

Love Out Loud

I've tried to love my life out loud
In a world of static silence.
I've tried to give more, love more,
BE more.
I've failed far more than I've succeeded.
No matter what else I've done in my life,
I've loved.
Not always wisely.
But always, ALWAYS, out loud.

The Silk Dress

A silk dress and cigarettes
With just a tired smile
She gladly took the walk of shame
In fact, she'd cling to it, awhile
She detoured to the beach, instead
Dug her toes into the sand
Felt the breeze up her silk dress
And thought, "Damn, I love that man."

The Poet

She really is magic
Her pen is her wand
Spins words into wisdom
Old soul from beyond
Like stars that still glitter
Though they've long turned to dust
She's so much to teach, still
But listen, you must
For words become faded
As years roll on past
Ink fades into paper
It's not meant to last
So look close, and listen
To the words that she writes
Her wisdom is timeless
Like stars in the night.

Stardust Inspiration

She's made of sunshine
With a heart of pure gold
The strength of archangels
And a warrior's soul
Her shield's made of wisdom
Her sword is her pen
She's sunshine, she's stardust
She's inspiration.

Every Woman

She smiles when her soul is breaking
Gets up when her whole body's aching
Takes care of her loved ones each night and each day
Fights the wolves at the door, though they howl, anyway
She keeps moving when all she wants is to drop
And hides in the shower when the tears just won't stop
Stares at the ceiling when sleep evades her most nights
And does it all again with each morning's light
She's stronger than even she knew she could be
She's every woman...she's you, and she's me.

Confusion

All too often, people confuse lust with love and call it hope.
And when reality calls in the marker,
They bleed inside their soul.
There may be beauty in letting go,
But only the strong survive.

Soul-Mates

She was the best thing that ever happened to him.
She was also the worst.
As was he, for her.
It wasn't until years later she realized that soul-mates
TRUE halves of the same,
Were separated for a reason.
Because, together,
One is the hydrogen that makes the other the bomb.

Fighting My Way Free

I smoke too many cigarettes,
And drink way too much caffeine.
Just to get through every moment
Without the urge to scream.
I hide inside the words I write,
Hoping nobody can see,
I'm not as strong as you think I am…

I'm just fighting my way free.

Acceptance

There's an emptiness in knowing
There's a life you'll never live
Dreams that slowly died to dust
Yet took all you had to give.
There's loneliness that's bigger
The Grand Canyon couldn't fill
While, even with crowds passing by,
Your soul is standing still.
Letting go of all you were
And all you'll never be
Acceptance is a bitch to find
And it DOESN'T set you free.

Goodbye

I made friends with Goodbye
A long time ago
She first grabbed my hand
When I was just 6 years old.
She's walked by my side
And whispered her creed
Every day, since,
That people all leave.
It's just how they are
And just what they do
Then she adds (very strongly)
It's them; it's not you.
See, Goodbye is my friend,
My sister of soul
And she's there to catch me
When each person goes.
So don't expect me to mourn you
I've no tears left to cry
I shed them all as a child
When I first met Goodbye.

Mandy Kocsis

Regrets

We lay in blankets of our regrets,
Cuddling them close
Like forgotten teddy bears.

Forever 44

You should've been 45, today
But Death walked you through her door
We should've been celebrating another year
Instead, you'll be forever 44.
It's not fair, and it hurts so much
Even months after you left
I still can't believe you're gone, now
I hope you found some peace in Death.
I can still hear you admonish me
That it's okay to ask for help
The fact that I didn't do just that,
Well, I'll never forgive myself
What I'd give to hear your voice
And feel your booming laughter
Just one more time, but it's far too late.
You're gone; that's all that matters.
You should've been 45, today
But you'll not age one day more
You'll live on in our memories…
Forever 44.

For My Brother
Matthew Thomas
11/29/73 - 9/27/18

A Million Goodbyes

I've had a hard life
There's much I'll not tell
Some moments were Heaven;
More moments were Hell
I don't say this for pity
You **did** ask me why
My eyes hold the pain
Of a million goodbyes
And that's nothing compared
To what's held in my heart
A million goodbyes
With no hello at the start.

I Hope You Understand

You were so much more than your ending
But that was long ago
Long before your alcoholic demons took your soul
Long before you lost yourself to the bottom of the wells
Long before we hit this fucking town that I call Hell.
You used to be a fighter, and a father, and a man
You used to be my husband, my lover, my best friend
Then alcohol, it changed you
Like Jekyll into Hyde
When I saw this day was coming
I left you, and I cried.
I should've left the first time Hyde put hands on me
I should've left the first time you left me to bleed
I tried so hard to save you; did everything I could
I hope some part of you inside understood
I hope you've finally found the peace you never really found
In the bottom of the bottle you built your life around
I hope that it was painless when the angels took you home
And I hope you finally understand just why I had to go.

For David R. Troxell
05/20/69 - 04/14/19

Grief Club

There's a grave that I don't visit
A tomb that I don't see
I lost her 20+ years ago
And I lost the best of me.
Don't ever let them tell you
How to get through each day
Most will never understand
And those that do, won't say
A club no one wants to be in
The price is just too steep
When the cost equals love lost
And lifetimes left to weep…
It even kills us in our sleep.

For Briana ShyAnne Kocsis
10/18/96 - 10/18/96

The Journey Home

Life is just the journey home
And at its end you die alone
Perhaps surrounded by ones who care
Still, in the end, it's just you there
Staring death straight in the eye
You spread your soul, alone, you fly
Watching days you lived go by
Softly telling life goodbye.

Life's the final bridge you'll burn
And, as you cross, you'll slowly learn
That you were never meant to stay
That souls are meant to fly away
A journey only you can make
Lessons only you can learn
Still, in the end, that bridge you'll burn.

Flames that light your soul on fire
Giving fuel to take you higher
Into the darkness that awaits
Alone is how you'll meet your fate
When you're landing at the final gate
None can join you; alone, you'll wait…

Mandy Kocsis

So make your journey count, my dear
For all too soon, the end is near
And before you know, it's time to go…

Life is just the journey home.

When Stars Go Dark

The Night's a little darker, now
The moon has lost her glow
The star that held your soul is dark
You found your way back home.
Your brilliance that lit up the night
Your shine that brought the day
Has left us more than lost inside
We've lost the light to guide the way
I hope that you've found peace at last
And I hope you're flying free
Tell the others that we love you all
And we'll miss you till we meet
Again.

Rest in Paradise, Courtney
5/2/93 - 2/24/20

So Much More To Me

I will forever and always be
"The girl who survived such adversity"
Forever and always I'll be known
As "she who threw back all life has thrown"
But there's so much more to me.
A lover of words since I was quiet young
Mother of the most amazing son
Daughter of the strongest woman alive
I'm so much more than "the girl who survived"
There's so much more to me.
Blessed to have found true love, again
In the arms of a rare (truly GOOD) man
Lover of unicorns and all things magic
Not all that makes me is dark and tragic

There's so much more to me.

Dangerous Beautiful

If Dangerous wasn't Beautiful,
Nobody would buy it.

Keep Your Therapy

Don't ask me to get therapy
The paper's always there for me
And though some words are hard to tell
The paper doesn't judge my Hell
It doesn't care how hard I cry
Or for who, or how, or why
Or if I'm an ice cold "nothing's there"
While throwing madness through the air
You can keep your therapy
I'll bleed into my poetry.

GPS

Until you've navigated through my mind
Don't tell me how to live my life.

Survival Guide

Do you know what it's like
To drown within your mind?
To be held captive by your soul?
Do you know what it's like to know
There's no final finish line,
No winning to this war
Some days it's not worth fighting for
Some days I'd give up everything
To lay down and breathe my last
But for my son I'd do just that.
Do you know what it's like
To fight demons night and day?
Forever bleed internally
Wounds that can never heal
And every single cut, you feel
Stuck on repeat, fall in defeat
Pull yourself to your feet
Just to fall back in the feels
Triggers everywhere
A word, a smell, a taste
Recreates that terror
Do you know? Do you?
I pray you never do

Don't judge until you've walked in my shoes
Feel free to bounce if it's too much for you
Goddess knows what I'd give to follow you
But this is my life
And all I can do,
Is survive.

Cosmic Twins

Burn it all down
Send flames in your wake
Till the smoke chokes the sound
Incompetence makes
And uncaring abounds
In this fake-ass fishbowl
We're all swimming around.

You told me once that I had changed
And I told you, you weren't the same
Both of us have drowned in pain
Again and again and again and again

We're too much alike
Cosmic twins till the end
Checkmate, pain-hike
And we're spinning, again

But of love and of words
I know this to be true
Nobody cared
As much as we, two

And I'll always be here
Forever, for you.

Bloody Love Memorial

Lessons learned
From memories earned
And nights spent bathed in blood
Pray you never know
How it breaks your soul
To escape death disguised as love.

Mandy Kocsis

Cloudy Dreams

She dreams in clouds of colors
But she lives in clouds
Of storms and thunder.

null

null

null

null

null

null

null

null

null

null

null

null

null

null

null

null

null

null

null

null

null

null

null

null

null

null

null

null

null

null

null

null

null

null

null

null

null

null

null

null

null

null

null

null

null

null

null

null

null

null

null

null

null

null

null

null

null

null

null

null

null

null

null

null

null

null

null

null

null

null

null

null

null

null

null

null

null

null

null

null

null

null

null

null

null

null

null

null

null

null

null

null

null

null

null

null

null

null

null

null

null

null

null

null

158

Dandelion Wish

Remember, oh, so long ago
When everything was love
Candy canes were magic wands
And dreaming was enough?
The future seemed so far away
When time was just a number
On a circle that you had to read
And angel's furniture was thunder
So long ago it's hazy, now
Even the memories are mist
Sometimes I think it wasn't real
Like a dandelion wish.

Neverland

And the wind in the willows
Through the wardrobe of my soul
The Lion and witch, they console me
When the darkness takes me whole
The sidewalk ends, for me, within
It's where the wild things are
For a wrinkle in time, things were different
But not since the second star
Then Neverland consumed me
Lost children aren't always found
And the Wizard tried to kill me
In life, I've often drowned
There's darkness in such tales not told
And some of us become them
Make me the Velveteen Rabbit, dear
It's best I be forgotten.

Changes

And the doubters became dreamers
While locked inside their homes
And the loners finally understood
They really weren't alone
While families came together
Like hadn't done in years
Playing games and making memories
And laughing through the tears
The world just kept on turning
And time ceased to exist
Making me think, maybe
We were meant to come to this.

Now is the Time

And when this is over
When this has passed
Let's come together
So much better, en masse
Let us remember
The lessons we've learned
This planet we live in
Isn't something we earned
A gift from the cosmos
A place we can live
And for our survival
Do better than this
Lay down your envy
Your self-driven greed
Spread love like a virus
Spread hope like a seed
When this is over
As it one day will be
Just hold one another
And set humanity free
From all of the chains
Anger, hatred, and rage
Leave them behind us

While we turn the next page
I know we can do it
There's no doubt in my mind
We just need to prove it
And now is the time.

Bottled Pain

I bottle pain like I breathe air
Without a second thought
And never let them see you cry
If they're the ones at fault
Has been my lifetime mantra
For as long as I recall
And I might bleed when I hit bottom
But won't tell who made me fall
If you're close enough to hurt me
If I've let you in that far
Then I can only blame myself
For my soul's new battle scars.

He Gave Me Rain

"Do you hear that?!" He said.
I looked at him and shook my head.
"Legally deaf, remember?" I grinned.
He went to the window and lifted the blinds. It was
storming like crazy outside.
"You don't hear that? The rain?" He asked.
"Babe, I haven't heard the rain since I was 9 years old."
I would be 39 in 2 weeks.
He grabbed his phone and started going through
YouTube channels of rain sounds till he found one I
could hear.

The man gave me rain. The sound of rain. To many,
that would be nothing. Laughed at, even. But to
me, it was nothing short of a miracle.

He's gone, now. I haven't listened to the rain since.
But sometimes, on days like today, I look out the
window at a storm, and I remember.

As even the Earth weeps.

Catastrophic

I loved you like a hurricane
Until you became the storm
Making landfall in my soul
With an eye to do me harm
A Cat-6 like there's never been
Tornadic winds sustaining
Pulling me apart inside
While trying to detain me
I loved you like a hurricane
Until you became the storm
Determined to destroy me
And I couldn't love you, anymore.

Here's to the difference
Between survival
And existence.

About the Author

Mandy Kocsis was born and raised in Detroit, Michigan; something she takes a lot of pride in. She's had a hell of a life, and often says, "if I can help one person with my words, just one, it all will have been worth it." Ms. Kocsis currently resides in Indiana with her son and her mother, who she cares for full time and is, she says, "the strongest woman I've ever known."

Manufactured by Amazon.ca
Bolton, ON